# From Wantrepreneur ™ To Entrepreneur

*Mindset Shift Blueprint to Your Divine Purpose*

By

## Jacqueline Turnbo, MBA

Vision Concepts, LLC
Columbus, OH 43219

Copyright © 2018 by Vision Concepts, LLC

All rights reserved. This book or any portion thereof may not be reproduced or used in any manner whatsoever without the express written permission of the publisher except for the use of brief quotations in a book review.

Edited by Julie Spangler

Printed in the United States of America

ISBN: 9781791792060

Vision Concepts, LLC
Columbus, OH
www.VisionConceptsBizConsulting.com
info@visionconceptsbizconsulting.com

# Dedication

*This book is dedicated to anyone on the fence about their purpose. It's time to accept who you were created to be. Trust and embrace the process and #LiveOnPurpose.*

# Thank You...

for purchasing this book. We would like to give you a gift. To claim it go to:
**bit.ly/bbizchecklist**
Don't forget to leave a review on Amazon.

# Table of Contents

Introduction ............................................................. 7

Chapter 1 - If Not Now, Then When? ........................ 11

Chapter 2 - Get Out of Your Head! ............................ 19

Chapter 3 - Oh Yeah, I DID Say That! ....................... 29

Chapter 4 - From Wantrepreneur™ To Entrepreneur ...... 33

Chapter 5 - It's Only Too Late When You Stop Breathing . 55

Chapter 6 - Making The Move, So What Now? ............ 63

Chapter 7 - Okay, I Changed My Mind...Let Me Off! ...... 71

Chapter 8 - Power Moves .......................................... 77

Chapter 9 - I'm Ready To Align .................................. 87

Chapter 10 - Mindset Blueprint of Your Divine Purpose .... 95

Conclusion ............................................................. 109

## *Introduction*

There is a process in becoming an entrepreneur. We are so quick to read "how to" books without realizing it requires a mindset shift, a whole new way of thinking. Yes, it can be a dream come true, but it can also be a nightmare if you don't face the responsibility that comes with owning a business and being an entrepreneur. Few people will be transparent about the harsh reality of the sacrifices. Instead, they will share their victories and the grandeur of being "your own boss." That has its place but what about the process better yet the mindset shift?

I wrote this book to help individuals shift their mindset before going into business, more importantly, embrace their purpose. Hopefully, their divine purpose. Yes, this book will have some insight on starting a business but it's more to help individuals grasp the need for a mindset shift before making one of the most important decisions one can make, taking a step towards their dream, goal, and vision.

Yes, it's a wonderful thing to have a vision and see it become a reality but it's important to know that the entrepreneurial journey is not a playground. Again, this book is not a "how to" book, it is a blueprint for a mindset shift, embracing and aligning with your purpose.

Ask yourself, are you willing to put in sweat equity? Meaning are you willing to get your hands dirty by putting in the work required to set up a sustainable, and profitable business model? How about implementing systems so, you can keep the promise to deliver your product/service? Entrepreneurship is not something you can enter lightly then expect a return on your investment. Let's be clear, if you do not put in the work you will not see results. Your time is valuable so make great use of it by shifting your mindset and positioning yourself to do what it takes to see your dream, goal, and vision manifest.

This book is also designed to lay the groundwork for a mindset shift. We can't allow our emotions to dictate our decisions in business. We must have a solid understanding of the what, when, where and how of our business. Yes, there are highs and lows, but we must be willing to ride the storm. We must be willing to set ourselves apart so the individuals we are assigned can find us. Therefore, we must be authentic in our vision and not fit in the crowd. We must maintain our integrity at all cost with no compromise because in the end, our actions will determine our outcomes. This book is not to deter you from pursuing dreams but to encourage you to embrace your dreams, goals, vision and hopefully align with your divine purpose. It's time to look at our lives and see what we were created to do. Let's not waste any more time.

Allow this book to help you go deep within and be honest about your intentions and your motives. May it help you be more determined to carry out your life's mission. We hope you gain the focus you need to begin moving towards your goal, dream, and vision. This is phase one of the Mindset Shift Blueprint to Your Divine Purpose.

# Chapter 1 - If Not Now, Then When?

Are you in a job or career that's not serving your passion? You may wonder what I mean by "serving your passion." Are you utilizing your gifts and talents directly related to the thing you love to do? The thing you love so much, you would almost be willing to do for free. Notice, I said "almost." If you find yourself unhappy at the thought of spending one more day doing a task rather than providing a product or service that will make a difference and positive impact, ask yourself how you will change your situation. Have you considered we all have an assignment, something we specifically are designed to do? There is purpose with your name on it, which is something your job or career cannot fulfill.

**Reality Check**

You may be telling yourself, "This 9 to 5 job isn't cutting it anymore." Are you truly living up to your fullest potential by staying on that job year after year? Many individuals are disengaged from their position. After a certain point, an uninspired job loses it savor. This is especially true if you're over the age of 35. With age, tolerance decreases. Whether it's dealing with the responsibility of management or simply dealing with different personalities. Job security is a thing of the past. Companies are downsizing in record numbers, outsourcing and eliminating positions more than ever. How secure is your future? Let's not mention your retirement benefits. What would you do if tomorrow you were given a box to pack your personal belongings and told you are laid off or your position has been eliminated? Or maybe you're thinking about retiring sooner than later. You may ask yourself, "What's next?"

Don't wait to think about this until something tragic happens or your funds are limited. Be proactive, prepare, and position yourself to invest in your future. Now is the time to discover your purpose and embrace it. Gain focus and pursue your passion and you just might find the very thing you were created to do. You can no longer depend on corporations to provide jobs that will last, with pensions to sustain you upon retirement. The reality is you must create products and/or services, build wealth and make a difference. It's time to be intentional in everything and live your best life, live on purpose. And how do you do that? Take the steps necessary to do what you are called to do. It is possible to concurrently create your own wealth by monetizing your passion while making a difference. Implement the five S's:

1. Surrender to your purpose.

2. Save money.

3.   Set goals.

4.   Seek help from a mentor, coach and/or consultant.

5.   Strategize.

*Surrender* to your purpose by acknowledging you have a specific desire that won't go away. The volume of the voice within is getting louder, asking "When will you move toward your purpose?" It's time to answer "Now!" See yourself doing something different, something you love, something that will make a difference to those you've been called to serve. This will require a shift in your mindset and openness to change.

*Save money*; you will need to invest in your vision and will need a source of income when you leave your job or retire. Budget your money now so you can invest later without it being a hardship. It is common knowledge that individuals looking to enter into entrepreneurship should save an equivalent of six to twelve months salary. This will provide a cushion when you decide to take that leap, or when your job decides they don't need you anymore. When starting a business, you may not see an immediate profit. During the first five years of opening a business, you will do well to break even, so be prepared. Entrepreneurship is not for the faint of heart.

*Set goals* so you can move forward; desire alone is not enough to put legs on your vision. You must have a plan, part of which requires you to have goals. Determine your goals, WHY you want to reach them and what action steps you need to take. Consistency and commitment are key elements needed in reaching or exceeding goals.

> *"A dream becomes a goal when action is taken toward its achievement."* ~ Bo Bennett

*Seek help from a mentor, coach and/or consultant;* this will help you develop and grow. Connecting with someone who is doing what you desire to do is inspiring and motivating. They can help clarify grey areas and provide insight. A mentor or coach may not be versed in every area of your industry/platform; however, you can glean from their experience.

*Strategize;* this is necessary when developing a business. It's important to be specific. Vital information and tactical methods are good components of a successful plan. Be intentional, your vision/dream/goal is not a random thought. You were created for a specific purpose. Don't minimize your gifts and talents. Acknowledge your untapped potential and purpose. There is something greater you were designed to do. Put in the work, do your research or hire Vision Concepts, LLC to help you. Vision Concepts, LLC enjoys helping individuals embrace and align with their divine purpose and develop strategic ways to monetize their passion. I am not suggesting you quit your job today! However, you must be honest with yourself. Do you want to live the rest of your days dreaming of how it would be to pursue your purpose, hopefully your divine purpose? It will require commitment, sacrifice and focus. There is a process, things you must put in place, with much preparation and planning. Most of all, you will need to be "deprogrammed" from an employee longing to be their own boss to becoming one. Or as I like to say, **"From Wantrepreneur™ to Entrepreneur."**

This is no small feat. You can't wake up one day, say "I think I want to own my own business, non-profit organization or head up a major community effort" and do it easy peasy. If you think you can, you're in for a rude awakening. Your organization will dissolve rather than evolve if your resolve is not more than a fuzzy feeling. Simply put, if your actions don't align with your divine purpose, you are setting yourself up for failure.

**List 10 Reasons Why You want to become an Entrepreneur.**

## Out of the 10 Reasons, what do you think will be the most challenging? Why?

# Chapter 2 - Get Out of Your Head!

*A*re you waiting for the right moment before you will take a step towards starting your business or pursuing a project? Maybe you are waiting for your ship to come in? Well my friend, you may be waiting for a long time if you're not setting goals and taking action. Do you know what your goals are? Have you made a plan? Do you even know why you want to pursue it? These are questions you need to ask yourself. Challenge yourself today, and be determined to follow through with your dream, vision or project. Be ACCOUNTABLE and TAKE ACTION!

Being an entrepreneur can be overwhelming. If you constantly second guess yourself, listening to the negative thoughts rolling around in your head will cause your vision to be cloudy, decrease your confidence and add stress. It's easy to convince yourself you may not have what it takes, or an idea will not work. But it takes courage to face obstacles and press through opposition. Sometimes the answer may be right in front of you. You can't see it if you're distracted by the noise in your head.

## Gain Perspective

Have you ever experienced a situation several times and wondered why it keeps re-occurring? Have you considered it may be happening to get your attention? Last year, I left my phone behind twice in a row. Once at the library and the other at a store. Both times, I was blessed enough to retrieve it. Needless to say, I gained some insight. The outcome could have been costly, but God in His Grace allowed me to get a lesson out of it. What event or mishap keeps occurring in your life that may be trying to get your attention? For me, the lesson was to be intentional and more conscience of my actions. Don't get so caught up in the hustle and bustle you aren't paying attention to what you're doing. The following three points are important:

1. **Take Time To Decompress**

Don't allow the cares of life to cloud your perception. Otherwise, you may do something that will bring your progress to a halt and cause you to lose momentum. For me, I believe my experience helped me realize the need to be still long enough to hear God's voice. To get into a quiet space, regain focus and clarity, listen to some music. I love soaking, worship music. What relaxes you?

2. **Be Deliberate**

Write your thoughts down, decompress, and be intentional about what you're doing. Don't get derailed or distracted. Keep purpose in mind when you're working on goals, but ensure you are including some down time. Be deliberate in your actions. There is a reason for everything.

## 3. Be Detailed

Pay attention to detail. Don't go through life wandering without purpose. Position yourself for the opportunities that will help get you get to your next level. There's a saying "The devil is in the detail." Well, I beg to differ and so does Gustave Flaubert. His quote is "God is in the detail." The devil will have you focusing on the wrong things whereas God will cause you to give attention to the very thing you need for the next step in your journey.

Avoid what I would like to call "Martha moments." You get so caught up in the event or problem you can't see the solution in front of you. This is derived from the story in the Bible when Martha was so overcome by her brother Lazarus dying, she didn't see this was an opportunity for Jesus to show His ability to do the miraculous. Don't allow anxiety to cause you to miss the opportunity that allows the solution to manifest. Remember, THERE IS A MESSAGE IN THE MISHAP.

> "To change ourselves effectively, we first had to change our perceptions." ~ Stephen Covey

**What are some of your negative thoughts discouraging you from perusing your dream, goals or vision? Get them out of your head so you can see how alarming they are in terms of your purpose.**

_____

_____

_____

_____

_____

_____

_____

_____

_____

_____

_____

_____

_____

**How will you disarm them? Hopefully with your actions. What actions steps will you take to achieve your goals in becoming an entrepreneur?**

_____

_____

_____

_____

_____

_____

_____

_____

_____

_____

_____

_____

_____

_____

_____

_____

**What mishap have you experienced that got your attention? What lesson did you learn from it?**

## How will you decompress?

## What will you be deliberate about personally and/or professionally?

## How will you give attention to detail concerning your pursuit in business?

From Wantrepreneur ™ To Entrepreneur

# Chapter 3 - Oh Yeah, I DID Say That!

Okay, you feel the pressure of your decision to take the leap and pursue your dream or vision, but you continue to think about the steps you must take. The closer you move toward your goals, the more distractions occur; you find yourself back in the old routine because you've decided you don't want to experience the pains of purpose. You take a dose of complacency, since it's easier to fade away into the norm and drown out the view of your vision than to listen to the voice of destiny calling you. What about the promise of pursuit you made? Face it, the struggle is real, we all have to face challenges and endure a transformation that doesn't always feel good.

I'm reminded of a time I took a walk and felt so excited to have the ability to walk on sidewalks, which had been considered a rare commodity in our neighborhood. Several months of major construction had occurred above- and below-ground to bring these precious sidewalks to us. I can remember how frustrating it was during the construction not having access to walk to the local park, but although the construction was inconvenient for our area during that time, it was for the betterment of the community.

I have a point to sharing this story. Sometimes we must undergo "construction" in order to move to the next level in our journey. We may be stretched beyond our comfort zone and not allowed access to familiar things. It doesn't always feel good. Some situations are self-inflicted; brought upon ourselves. Sometimes God allows us to go through situations, so we can grow, be postured, and be shaped into the person He desires.

Just as the construction in my neighborhood included many unseen improvements to the infrastructure, God is working to improve the inside of you. You'll have a greater infrastructure. Actually, it's been there all along, according to His divine plan. It's being manifested in due time. When He propels you into your next phase, you'll be ready to sustain what He's doing in your life.

Be encouraged, in whatever you're enduring right now. If you're doing something that's extremely difficult and you're thinking, "How much longer will I have to go through this?" Think about the end result. You'll be better for it. Remember what you said... Your destiny is counting on it.

> *"Begin with the End in Mind."* ~ Stephen Covey

**What are some areas you need to develop in? Be honest with yourself.**

## What will you do to shift your thinking?

# Chapter 4 - From Wantrepreneur™ To Entrepreneur

Entrepreneurship is not for the faint of heart. You must determine if you are a leader. If so, do you have the ability to lead yourself? If you can't lead yourself, how can you expect to lead others? You may say, "What do you mean, lead yourself?" Well, are you practicing what you preach? Are you doing what you expect others to do? Never take the attitude "Do as I say and not as I do." Being an entrepreneur means you report to no one. If you screw up, you're the one who will have to deal with it. Since this is the case, let me ask you the following:

- Are you consistent?
- Are you accountable for your actions?
- Do you know why you're doing what you do?
- Are you willing to make a difference?
- Is your integrity intact?

- Are you willing to continue to develop personally, and professionally?

- Can you take constructive criticism without being offended or becoming defensive?

- Do you have faith despite what you see; good or bad? (mustard seed faith Matt. 17:20 NIV)

- Will you follow through on commitments?

- Will you invest in YOU?

These are simply a few things you need to ask yourself before embarking on your own business venture. Also, you can no longer have the mindset of an employee; working for the weekend and expecting a bi-weekly paycheck or salary. Guess what! If you don't put the time in and/or potential customers/clients don't buy into your product or service, you won't get paid. Even if you do get paid, this money will now be working capital for your business. There is no guarantee of immediate profit. I've learned to face this hard reality daily. In the initial start-up, a small business owner may not see a profit for the first few years. [1]

A higher level of commitment is required in being an entrepreneur. A mindset shift must take place as you push past the questions: What if? What am I doing? Is this going to work? Maybe this wasn't such a good idea? An entrepreneur must have the wherewithal to generate their business. Entering business is not something one should

---

[1] https://www.bls.gov/careeroutlook/2014/article/self-employment-what-to-know-to-be-your-own-boss.htm

enter blindly with only a "good idea." Once you've discovered you can lead yourself and the level of commitment is there, setting attainable goals are necessary. Begin to focus on and complete the following:

- Develop a sound business model.

- Research your market.

- Determine your target audience.

- Conduct a SWOT (i.e., strengths, weaknesses, opportunities, threats) analysis. (See example at the end of this chapter).

- Create a marketing strategy.

- Create a business plan.

- Acquire licensures/registrations with the Secretary of State (in your State).

- Research industry compliance requirements of your local government.

- Acquire Liability Insurance/Bonding (if required by your industry).

- Develop a strong team.

- Find Advisers who can guide you in the process (e.g., Lawyer, Accountant, Business Consultant).

- Build your audience by showing how your product/service can solve their problem.

- Gain trust.

- Develop your company's social media presence.

- Start a blog.

- Stay in touch with your industry.

- Network at conferences or other events.

- Read articles, blogs and other information relevant to your field.

- Continue Personal Development.

- Keep a good attitude and maintain your spiritual life.

- Balance home and business.

- Obtain a mentor(s) who's doing or has done what you desire to do.

- Read personal development books.

There is much more to business and becoming an entrepreneur than we realize. Taking the lead and searching ourselves to see what we're made of is a good beginning to becoming an effective leader.

We've covered the business side, but there are also personal financial investments for the wellbeing of you and your family you need to consider:

- Life insurance and Annuities.
- Retirement.
- Health insurance.
- Securing your assets (e.g., homeowners' insurance/rental insurance).
- Car insurance.
- Monthly living expenses.

If your job provides life and health insurance, do you know how much it would cost to keep similar insurance if you decide to leave your job? How about your retirement plan, 401k, Roth IRA, etc. Do you have stock options? Are you going to roll over your retirement into another plan? Do you have savings/emergency fund? These are items you need to assess prior to leaving your current position. Don't take the attitude "Oh, I'll cross that bridge when I come to it," or "I can't deal with that right now, there are too many other things for which to be concerned." These may be long-term topics, but trust and believe if you don't make decisions and take action now, it will have an adverse effect on your short-term. You don't want to be like an ostrich, sticking your head in the sand and hoping all will be better when you emerge. And, you don't want to be like a deer in headlights, being caught by surprise or freezing at every turn. Be a tactician of your own Destiny.

## There's A Greater Plan

Whatever you are pursuing, be consistent in your endeavors and shift your mindset. It requires determination to complete goals/projects. You can, if you're committed and have a plan. Speaking of a plan, I'm reminded of a time while watching the Daystar Television Network and their founder Marcus Lamb, reading scriptures while preaching his message concerning the crucifixion of Jesus. He illustrated the whole scenario by stating, "God spoke to his spirit and said, "I planned it." When Jesus came and sacrificed His life, all of it was planned for you." If God, with His infinite knowledge, put a plan in place, how much more do WE need a plan?

That's confirmation of what's been resonating in my spirit. We must be serious about putting plans and strategies in place concerning the things God is calling us to do and be committed no matter what! Let me be transparent. It's not easy when you're trying to follow the vision God has given you. Sometimes, you may want to throw up your hands and say, "It was a good idea, but I am tired." However, if we put a plan in place, commit to prayer and walk in the direction God has given us, we can see progress. Allow yourself to be open to those individuals God has put along your path to help you. It will take investing in the things we need to do for development of systems/processes we want to implement in our business and platforms.

As I've said before, it's not always going to be easy, but it will be worth it in the end. If we can touch one, two, even three people, it will be worth it, #liveonpurpose. That's our motto. Whatever you're doing, create a plan, commit to prayer, be committed and determined that you're going to see it through. So, if you're writing books, blogs, building your platform, whatever you're doing, it will happen. It will come to fruition. God will bless your vision as you shift your mindset and embrace your divine purpose. Decide you will do what it takes to succeed and effectively serve those you've been assigned to serve.


## Information is Power

As an entrepreneur, I realize the importance of having crucial information in my decision-making processes. It motivates me to provide business research and development strategies for clients/business partners. My goal is to help position them to meet or exceed their goals. I know all too well about having wrong information or not having enough facts prior to venturing into the unknown. Don't be left in the dark by assuming you have all the facts. Knowing the when, where, how and WHY, can save you time and money. Once you've determined these factors, you're ready to proceed.

Here's a word to the wise before speaking to a perspective buyer or seller, prepare a list of questions to ask. Don't be shy, you won't know unless you ask. Know the time frame you need the product or service and stick to it. Don't put yourself in a position that makes you unable to deliver. Stick to your budget, but don't compromise on quality. If you do, you will end up paying much more to get what you need. It's a process in producing your vision, dream or idea. Remember to enjoy the journey.

Do you want to be an entrepreneur of opportunity? One who brings value, giving clients the opportunity to flourish in their space; or an entrepreneur of importunity, causing prospective clients to run in the other direction because you're trying to push your product or service on them instead of showing how you bring value to their space. Check your motivation and ask yourself why you do what you do. Be intentional; create a system or product you know can make a difference to others. This will help strengthen your chances of winning the sale, gaining the contract or being awarded a project. Allow it to open the door of opportunity to provide a product or service of value. In turn, you may form a long-term relationship with your client. Gain leverage produce profitability and promote sustainability with a viable approach to entrepreneurship.

## We Are Destined for Greatness

We are designed to be change agents on the earth, encouraging people to live their purpose and walk in purpose while living their fullest potential and accomplishing the things God has created them to do.

If we're not in a right relationship with our Heavenly Father, all of this is for nothing. It's important to line up with Him and what He says for your life. Align with His plan, because only His plan will prevail or succeed. If we follow this course, there's no stopping us. You know the goals, dream and vision you have, I encourage you to move forward, line up with your Creator and He will give you the resources you need because He is your source.

> *"Many are the plans in a person's heart, but it is the LORD's purpose that prevails."* ~ *Proverbs 19:21 NIV*

## Strategic Insight

Below is an example of a SWOT Analysis. You should conduct an analysis to determine the position of your company (even in its conception stage) in comparison to competitors in your industry. What strengths does your company provide? What weaknesses does your company have? What opportunities do you have to use as leverage? What threats do your competitors present and/or what threats do you present to them?

You can also conduct an analysis of your mindset towards your purpose. What are your strengths? How positive are you? What are your weaknesses in achieving goals? What opportunities of personal development do you have in terms of pursuing your vision? What are some behaviors that pose as a threat in achieving your dream, goals, vision? Conduct a business and personal SWOT analysis today.

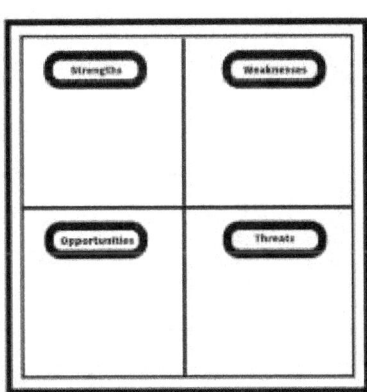

**Are you consistent? If not, why?**

**Be honest, are you accountable for your actions? If not, what is your first course of action to make a change?**

**Is your integrity intact? Meaning, are you open to compromise? If yes, why?**

**Do you know why you're doing what you do? Write some things down to remind yourself.**

_____

_____

_____

_____

_____

_____

_____

_____

_____

_____

_____

_____

_____

_____

_____

_____

**Are you willing to make a difference? Why do you have a passion for your vision?**

**Are you willing to continue to develop personally and professionally? Name some programs that would benefit your growth? If you don't know, research your industry and write them down.**

_____

_____

_____

_____

_____

_____

_____

_____

_____

_____

_____

_____

_____

_____

_____

## Can you take constructive criticism without being offended or becoming defensive? If not, why?

**Do you have faith despite what you see; good or bad? (mustard seed faith Matt. 17:20 NIV) What does mustard seed faith mean to you?**

_____

_____

_____

_____

_____

_____

_____

_____

_____

_____

_____

_____

_____

_____

_____

# From Wantrepreneur ™ To Entrepreneur

**Will you follow through on commitments? If not, why? If yes, describe a commitment you kept. How did it make you feel?**

**Will you invest in YOU? Will you invest in a mentor or coach? If not, why?**

# Chapter 5 - It's Only Too Late When You Stop Breathing

*N*ever give up on your dreams. Don't allow someone's "no" to determine your level of motivation. You were created for a purpose. That "no" may help steer you in the right direction, putting you closer to your destiny. Challenges and opportunities can fuel the creativity necessary to achieve goals. It will take work on your part to press through discouragement and fear of failure. Operate in faith not fear. Your success is waiting for you on the other side of "no."

## Are You Committed?

Have you ever been hacked? The reason I ask is because in early 2018 my website was hacked not once but twice. We were launching new workshops and had scheduled a Canva 101 Workshop[2] the same week. We had committed to do at least one Canva workshop a month, and this was the first workshop of the year. Access to all the registration information was on my website. As the week progressed, I didn't create a backup plan in time to meet my goal. Needless to say, the workshop didn't happen. During this same time, I was also dealing with personal issues. The point of the story, there was one opposition after the other. That's why I asked the question, have you ever been hacked. Does it seem as if you take two steps forward and are then pushed back three? Better yet, allow me to ask, are you committed to what you started? Are you committed to your goals? Are you committed to your dreams even though difficult situations arise? Trust me, at some point life will happen; you must be determined and press on.

While going through this adversity, I watched a video of Priscilla Shirer about discerning God's voice. One of the things that resonated with me was her mention of aligning with God's divine purpose. When she said that, my antennas went up. God must position us or align us. He wants to make sure we're in alignment with His purpose, what He's calling us to do. Priscilla Shirer told the story of her days in gymnastics and how there were certain things her coach would look for during practice. If she wasn't positioned or aligned correctly, he wouldn't release her to do certain moves. This was especially true if Pricilla's head and back weren't in position. She went on to say, this is how God does when He has something for us to do. He wants to make sure we're in alignment with His will, and many times things will

---

[2] http://visionconceptsbizconsulting.com/canva-101-power-of-diy-workshop/

happen to show us where we are. Pricilla Shirer also talked about the position of the heart.

If your heart is postured to hear God's voice and discern what He's calling for despite circumstances, are you willing to get in divine alignment? It may not feel good; even though things seem like they keep coming at you, you can rest in God's word. Your trust and faith will kick in and, without a shadow of a doubt, you will continue. Things I faced that week let me know the position of my heart. I encourage you to take time to allow God to show you where your heart is and if you're in alignment with His divine purpose. This is necessary to ensure you won't go through the rest of the year questioning or guessing along your journey.

## Truth Can Lead You To Divine Purpose

My story, I am a product of job displacement; it has been eight years. Thank God, He whispered new beginnings in my spirit as the eighth year approached. The number eight means new beginnings. I was employed for almost 24 years and didn't realize how much that job was a crutch. Don't get me wrong, I'm grateful for the experience and learned a lot. However, prior to my displacement, I felt prompted to leave but was too comfortable receiving a bi-weekly paycheck. My last few years in that job were miserable because I knew it was time to move on but didn't. When I was let go, it was actually a blessing in disguise.

Instead of aligning and positioning my heart with God's leading, I struggled. Now, here I am eight years later, finally developing into the person He's called me to be. That's why my mission and purpose is to encourage individuals to embrace their divine purpose. You can purpose to do so many things, so why not purpose to do that which God created you? You will save so much time. You will have so much fulfillment. It's never too late. As long as you have breath in your body, all you need is a willingness to open your heart and the commitment to what God is calling you to do. If you're not quite sure what He's created you for or if you don't know Him as your personal Lord and Savior, I encourage you to accept Him in your heart (Romans 10: 9-10 NIV and John 3:16 NIV).

Whatever it is that you truly believe you are supposed to do, you can do it with God on your side. Stop second guessing yourself; you are unique. You are the apple of His eye (Psalm 17:8 NIV). God loves you so much and He wants to have a personal relationship with you. He has a special plan for your life according to Jeremiah 29:11 NIV. He knows what it will take for you to be the best you can be, trust Him today. No matter what pressure you're facing, acknowledge God, position your heart to hear His voice. You'll get direction and be led down the right path.

> *"Life has no limitations except the ones you make."*
> *~ Les Brown*

**List your area(s) of research regarding your potential business or project. When do you plan on getting started? Write down some timelines for various areas of your planning.**

_____

_____

_____

_____

_____

_____

_____

_____

_____

_____

_____

_____

_____

_____

# Chapter 6 - Making The Move, So What Now?

*N*ow that you've pushed pass your doubts, you may be faced with family and friends questioning your motives. If you're married or in a relationship, a caregiver or single parent, you will need to have a conversation with your loved ones. You will receive push back in some form or another. It's important to keep your focus. There will be changes in your availability, which will affect them directly; both you and your loved ones will need to adjust. Don't allow them to make you feel guilty. There needs to be understanding from both parties. Think it through, have your plan prepared to share with them. Remember, they can't see your vision like you can.

It's time to set some goals and make sure you have an exit strategy in place. You can be proactive while you're still at your job and be ready to act on the steps we mentioned in chapters one and four. It's important to manage your time effectively. Commit to your schedule by making a list of action items you will complete each week. Commit to spending at least 20 hours on your business per week. During initial start-up, you'll need to treat it like a second job. Research is required; forming your business structure and planning is essential. You'll need a business plan, marketing plan and financial strategy plan.

At this point, your mindset shift will need to occur and renewed thinking will need implemented in your behavior. There's no turning back. The process will be overwhelming, but you can get through it if you don't allow negativity to set in. It helps to surround yourself with individuals of like mind to help support your entrepreneurial mindset. However, you still need to maintain your family and spiritual life. A healthy balance is a must. You will be tempted to revert to your old way of thinking when the pressure hits. Resist the feeling! Your emotions may be all over the place; if you ride the storm, the seas will eventually calm.

## Be Ready To Shift

Again, I'm reminded of the construction in my neighborhood. The entrance to my direct street was closed during the second half of the construction. I live near the gated city maintenance equipment yard. Normally, you can't get through, but due to the construction, they opened their gate for access to the back street. Prior to this detour, I never knew about that street. Just like experiencing a detour during construction, change takes place in our own lives. You grow accustomed to doing something a certain way and there's a glitch requiring a different direction. Okay, you make the change and take the detour.

I became accustomed to the detour, using the back road, just following the rules. When the main road finally reopened, I tended to look in the direction of the detour and realized I'd gotten used to going that way. I'll admit, it was more convenient. Few people enjoy the inconveniences of a detour. However, the detour allows you to discover things you may not have known if you hadn't gone down that path. It stretches you and makes you grow.

We can get comfortable with the change and think to ourselves, "I can roll with this." Then lo and behold, you don't need that detour anymore. As I looked towards the detour, the Holy Spirit whispered to me and said, "You don't need that detour; that was only for the time that you needed it. You don't need it anymore. The detour is closed."

The new road has much more access. It's amazing how different our area is now. In life, you'll have access to greater things if you keep moving forward. When you want to turn back, think to yourself "the detour is closed." You don't need those things you were holding onto, things for which you've become accustomed. Don't be comfortable in the shift. Learn what you need and keep moving forward; it was good for that season. God has so many things for you. He's elevating you to a whole new level. Be open to Him as you experience additional shifts and make more adjustments. Don't get stagnant; continue to grow and develop. We're all called for a specific reason. He knows the path we must take, and He knows our end result. It's all good because God keeps His promises.

Individuals are waiting on you to show up. You may not stay in one area, as you may be called to minister to others. There's someone else who needs your product/service, so don't be stagnant. The Path is open now. You must go a different direction.

## Sudden Moves Won't Make You Great

There are times when things don't seem to be moving fast enough and you may worry you will be forgotten. Especially if you're building platforms. Allow this extra time to help you gain perspective. For example, have you ever wondered what happened to an old classmate, teacher, a pillar in your community or a movie star? Like the saying "out of sight, out of mind" implies, if you don't see or hear about someone, they become an afterthought. We live in a social media-oriented society. One may assume because a person is not trending on social media or in the limelight of traditional media, nothing significant is occurring in their life.

A few years ago, my husband and I were looking at a few videos from the 1980's. We were focused on a particular family, who shall remain nameless. A few of their siblings became world renown and are current even now. We began to research a specific member of this celebrity family and discovered they had created wealth in their youth; while the spotlight was/is on their other siblings. Today this low-key celebrity is worth millions. Need I mention, this family member illustrates the most stability of all their siblings. Why am I mentioning this? Your actions speak louder than your visibility. What you do behind the scenes to prepare for short- and long-term goals, whether in business or personal, is what matters. You can trend or be in the spotlight and become famous, successful, even LARGER THAN LIFE, but if you don't lay a firm foundation and invest your time and talents in what's important (i.e., your spiritual and physical health/wellness, your family and your business), none of it matters. The celebrity I referred to earlier now has a well-rounded life, advocating an illness of a family member by providing invaluable information to others with this disease and building on a legacy. Their children are following suit.

Take some time to evaluate your life. It's ok to get attention but it's even better to position yourself and your business to make a difference. Let your ACTIONS SPEAK LOUDER.......

*"True progress quietly and persistently moves along without notice." ~ Saint Francis de Sales*

**List some things you want to share in the conversation with your loved one regarding your vision.**

_____

_____

_____

_____

_____

_____

_____

_____

_____

_____

_____

_____

_____

_____

# Chapter 7 - Okay, I Changed My Mind... Let Me Off!

When you decide to step out on faith and pursue your vision, you will feel the pressure of your decision and may begin to second guess yourself. The highs and lows of shifting to the entrepreneurial journey may feel like you're on a roller coaster. Imagine you decide to get on the scariest ride at an amusement park. The idea seems fun at first, but once you sit in the seat, the adrenalin rush is too overwhelming and causes you to have a change of heart. You think to yourself, "I changed my mind; let me off NOW!" You may even bellow it out. Your destiny isn't a mere amusement ride where you can change your mind and it's irrelevant. If you walk away from the opportunity of reaching your next level, you will regret it. Just think, your message, product or service could benefit others and solve their problem. If you don't follow through with your vision, others could be prevented from going to their next level. Don't be the missing link.

## Will You Leave A Strong Legacy?

Last year, a dear friend and sister in Christ suddenly passed away. This was extremely sobering; making me realize just how precious life is and how important it is to manage our time wisely. We must live on purpose, because you don't know how many people you may affect. She was a pillar of her community and left a strong legacy. Will others be able to say the same about you? Let's be obedient to the call on our lives. We can make a difference. Don't allow frustration, fear or defeat to make you forfeit your divine purpose.

Frustration will cloud your vision. Something simple can seem so difficult. You may be tempted to give up on your vision because you can't quickly figure things out or things aren't going according to plan. I can remember a time when I purchased a selfie light and there were no detailed instructions. The light wouldn't turn on no matter how hard I tried. Just when I thought it was a bad purchase, I noticed a little compartment on the back. I couldn't get it open, so I gave it to my husband. He opened it with no problem and, low and behold, it needed batteries!

The moral of the story is don't assume something is not right for you just because it's not going the way you think it should. God opens doors for a reason; you must be courageous and trust Him for guidance in your assignment. Just because you can't figure it out right away doesn't mean it isn't working. As I needed help opening the compartment, you may need someone to help you along your entrepreneurial journey.

If you need a mentor, seek a coach, accountability partner or someone who is doing what you desire to do. They can encourage you. Don't give up. You may just need to reframe the situation. It may not be as bad as you think. Learn lessons from each step in your journey. Again, don't be so quick to give up, the answer is right there. Take the extra step and get help.

> *If you're going to live, leave a legacy. Make a mark on the world that can't be erased." ~ Maya Angelou*

**List at least five reasons why you want to be an entrepreneur and how you want to make a difference.**

_____

_____

_____

_____

_____

_____

_____

_____

_____

_____

_____

_____

_____

_____

_____

Jacqueline Turnbo

# Chapter 8 - Power Moves

Starting a business can be overwhelming. Many components are involved in setting up a business model. A startup must be given attention to detail to promote profitability and sustainability. It's an uphill battle that includes complying with local and federal government requirements, maintaining working capital and managing your time. It's important to focus on your goal(s), recognize the need of total commitment to your business/vision and COMMIT. Don't allow yourself to become paralyzed by the unknowns. Keep moving forward. Take risks but don't be in the dark; if you fail, fail forward. Turn your challenges into opportunities. Always be open to new ideas for potential products and services, but don't move too fast.

As I've said before, don't be afraid to seek help. Individuals with knowledge and expertise are available to help you move to the next level. Build a solid infrastructure having the capacity to withstand the hardships in business and any future expansion. The following are power moves you must implement to solidify your position as an entrepreneur:

- Know your market – RESEARCH (Vision Concepts, LLC can assist you with a market analysis)[3]

- Build Relationships - gain trust from your client and build a strong team

- Plan for success - have the right information to help prevent pitfalls along the way

- Develop strategies and implement them – marketing, social media, effective systems

- Partner with the right partners – suppliers/vendors or subcontractors

- Don't compromise your credibility

- Know your numbers - your financials are not a guessing game, you want a positive yield on your investment

- Invest in yourself via a Mentor or Coach

- Remember SOME **A-C-T-I-V-I-T-Y** is better than none

>    **A**ccountability
>    **C**ommitment
>    **T**ime Management
>    **I**nvest
>    **V**alue yourself and Relationships
>    **I**mplement
>    **T**arget Market is important
>    **Y**ield

---

[3] http://visionconceptsbizconsulting.com/services-2/

In a previous chapter, I asked if you were a business of opportunity or importunity, either way you will be operating from capacity or scarcity. Hopefully, your foundation is based on capacity. However, a company may have capacity to supply their customers with products or services yet lack a personal touch. As an entrepreneur, we can't afford to neglect our Business to Customer (B2C) relationships. Our customers/clients aren't dollar signs, but people with needs and wants that can be fulfilled by our competitors. We can't get too comfortable by simply supplying products, meeting deadlines or exceeding goals. Our customers need our UNDIVIDED attention. If you're unsure of how to make a connection, take time to make conversation; be genuine and you may discover a mutual interest. Send greeting cards or acknowledgments. Handwritten thank you cards give a personal touch in this "digital age."

Acknowledge and address the customer/clients concerns immediately. Periodically, take a survey to see if the same concerns are common among patrons. The feedback is valuable data to position your company to provide improved service offerings for your customers/clients. Implementation of a CRM - Customer Relationship Management (email marketing/management system) is crucial to eliminate ineffective operations. Remember, without customers/clients you can't conduct business and attain profitability. More importantly, how can you add value to others when you have nobody to serve? Automation will help you stay on top of customer relations.

## Position Yourself for The Shift

While you're in the process of shifting into entrepreneurship, begin to develop a budget to make purchases to help run your business. Also, be proactive in securing your personal finances. The following are power moves you can make on a personal level that will help you invest in your business and position you to make the ultimate move; however, these should only be implemented if you have a business plan in place and a strategy to repay yourself quickly:

Investment Ideas *(Disclaimer: The following are just suggestions. We do not recommend you act on any of these investment ideas if you are not disciplined enough to reinvest and replace all monies used from any of these resources.)*

- Borrow against your 401k – only a small amount; have a plan to pay it back immediately

- Obtain a home equity loan - only use amount needed to assist you in your business; have a plan to pay it back immediately

- Evaluate your stock options - consider cashing some out (seek advice on reinvestment options)

- Purchase a CD (Certificates of Deposit) while you decide on your retirement strategy post-job

## Short-Term and Long-Term Financial Goals

- Refinance your mortgage for a lower interest rate

- Make principal payments on your mortgage every month

- Pay off bills now - use the amount you save towards another bill until they're all paid off

- Be aggressive investing into a retirement 401k - this will help you maintain your current lifestyle when you retire

- Cultivate discipline for your spending habits

- Save for business expenses

- Create a savings account (like a Christmas Fund) with limited access

- Invest in a Virtual Assistant - start out with a few days a week to work on small tasks

- CRM (Customer Relationship Management)/Email Management (Automation) System – sends emails to existing/potential clients/customers automatically

- HOSTING (a company that houses/stores your website)

- Website (you can begin to create content/ad copy for your website)

- P.O. Box or Membership for a monthly business incubator (use as business address)

- Refer to Biz list (Gift for purchasing this book)[4]

- Software such QuickBooks (you will need an accounting system in place to help track your expenditures)

- Upgrade plugins for WordPress site (upgrade plugins will enhance your website functionality-highly recommend WordPress based websites as they have more flexibility and you create multiple pages good for landing/sales pages)

- Domain names (there's an annual fee to keep the name of your website)

These are just a few ways you can leverage your business and personal finances. What you do today can make a world of difference tomorrow.

> "The past cannot be changed. The future is yet in your power." ~ Unknown

---

[4] http://bit.ly/fwtegift4U

**List your short-term goals.**

## From Wantrepreneur ™ To Entrepreneur

**List your long-term goals.**

# Chapter 9 - I'm Ready To Align

The power of choice is compelling. You can choose your own path, but is that better than following the path for which you were created? Often, what you're really doing is following a path someone else designed. You may be living the dream of your parents or loved ones while they live vicariously through you. Their intentions may be good, but is that better than what God has intended for you? Or, you may be rebellious and determined no one will tell you what do or how to live. In that rebellion you make choices that take you far from your journey of divine design. Some of you choose to play it safe and refuse to take a risk, but deep inside you long for more.

Not everyone has the resolve of a higher power capable of divine design. Consider the intricacy in human design alone; there must be a power far greater than our minds can fathom. The beauty of divine design is we have a choice to acknowledge God, yield to His leading and accept the plan He has for our lives. It's amazing to me. He's the Divine Architect with all power in His hand yet allows us to choose our own path. However, we don't have the capability nor sovereignty to see the future. Therefore, we should not rely on our own strength and run the risk of getting it wrong and wasting precious time. Time is one thing we can never get back. Why pursue something not relevant to our divine purpose?

I encourage you to choose wisely and align with God's plan for your life. It will not be easy. You may battle with loved ones, friends, foes or yourself, which is the toughest battle. You may think you have the answers as you experience pitfalls along the way but trust the plan God has for you and come into alignment with it.

## You Were Created on Purpose

One day, I had an "Aha!" moment. While listening to the radio, the announcer stated that Nick and Kanae Vujicic were expecting twins. Nick is a motivational speaker and author with an awesome platform called "Life without Limbs." You may wonder what is so significant about these people having children. Just humor me for a few moments. Nick has no limbs, but that doesn't stop him from carrying out the mission God has assigned to him. Nick Vujicic lives what he teaches and preaches as he travels around the world. His life is a living testimony that God can do anything.

What if Nick had given in to his situation, and having no arms or legs, continued to feel sorry for himself? Instead, he chose to be a vessel that God could use to reach millions of people around the world. He is the epitome of living on purpose and proof we were created on purpose. God created him the way he is for a reason. Countless people have come to the Kingdom of God by hearing his story. However, my "Aha!" moment came while thinking of the role his wife, Kanae, plays in their journey. She is proof that we were created on purpose. If Kanae had seen Nick and said, "Oh, I feel sorry for Nick. He seems like a nice guy, but I can't see a life with someone like him," and moved on, she would've missed an amazing life and love designed specifically for her. No, God created Kanae to be Nick's helpmate, the woman who will bear his children and continue his lineage. Kanae could have chosen another path but she didn't. She came into alignment with the path God had predestined for her.

God created Kanae on purpose, for Nick. Sidebar, if you're waiting on a mate, know that God created you and that person on purpose. He designed you for each other. Wait on him/her and be in position so you can connect. The point of this story, we were created on purpose for a specific reason and must align with our divine destiny. Kanae Vujicic came into alignment with her divine purpose and is fulfilling her destiny; you should do the same.

It's important to gain your focus and align with your divine purpose so you can be the person who God called you to be. Individuals are waiting on you to show up. One of Vision Concepts, LLC's mantras is that you were created on purpose. If you haven't started to move forward towards your goals, dreams and vision, do it today. If you don't know what your purpose is, it's time to find out. It will take commitment on your part. There is much fulfillment in knowing you are following the path created for you. Start with setting goals, which encourages discipline you will need on your entrepreneurial journey. Change your mindset by focusing on your goals and taking action.

## Tips to Gain Focus on Your Goals

We can't go aimlessly throughout the day and expect to achieve our goals. It's important to be intentional in all we do. Determine the objectives for your vision and how you will achieve your goals. Achieving goals is like hitting a target. You can only do that by maintaining your focus. The following are tips to help you maintain focus on your goals:

**PREPARE SUNDAY NIGHT**

> Plan out your week every Sunday night. Preparation helps reduce stress. You'll have a visual of your goals, something to work toward without going around in circles and accomplishing nothing.

**OBTAIN SUPPORT**

> Do you have a support system that will help you stay motivated? You need people who will help build you up and encourage you to keep going. How about an Accountability Partner? Be aware of your environment; surround yourself with individuals who are equally committed to reaching their goals. Join the Your Accountability Group (free closed Facebook Group).[5]

---

[5] http://bit.ly/yaccountability

## RECORD IMPORTANT FACTS

Avoid the frustration of forgetting ideas. Record your concepts on a voice recorder or mobile phone. You can also record important dates and prepare your weekly schedule.

## MINIMIZE DISTRACTIONS

Don't waste time by aimlessly watching television. Time wasted is less time you have to work on your goals and objectives. The same applies to social media, engaging in needless conversations and other misuses of time spent not serving your purpose. You get the idea.

## JOURNAL CONSISTENTLY

You would be amazed how writing in your journal consistently can help you maintain your focus. It helps you gain clarity by releasing all the clutter in your mind. It's also therapeutic, a stress reliever. Hit the target of your goals with commitment, discipline and focus. Most importantly, align with your divine destiny and watch God's plan for you unfold. You've got this!

> *"Trust in the Lord with all your heart, and do not lean on your own understanding. In all your ways acknowledge him, and he will make straight your paths. Be not wise in your own eyes; fear the Lord, and turn away from evil."* ~ *Proverb 3:5-7 ESV*

**Are you rebelling against your divine purpose? If so, how?**

# Chapter 10 - Mindset Blueprint of Your Divine Purpose

The Hoover Reservoir in Westerville, Ohio, is a local fitness attraction, with a steep set of ninety-eight stairs along each side of the dam. A few years ago, I decided to work on my goal to climb these steep stairs a total of five times. Well, I didn't reach my goal, but I did climb them twice and am determined to conquer them - eventually.

If you don't reach a goal, take a step back, reassess, come up with a strategy, and then go back and try it again. With my stair goal, I located some other stairs I know I can climb, and I'm going to master those stairs. At that point, I'll return to Hoover Reservoir's steep stairs and attempt to climb them five times or more. Go for whatever goals you have, whatever strategies you need to implement; it's time to do it. If you don't quite reach your goal, step back and reassess, come up with a strategy plan, implement that strategy and conquer, meet or exceed your goals. You can do it.

The challenges of life can cause you to group everything into one category. Priorities may get lost in the mix. It's easy to lose focus and miss opportunities of a lifetime that will create memories and help transform lives. Long-term goals can be placed at the bottom, causing one to lose sight of the future. Take some time to analyze your life and give every area the proper attention. The investment of time spent now to prioritize and make proper assessments will help you receive a greater yield on your returns in the future.

## Take Action Now

What does it mean to 'build' your business? You are on the right track by taking action NOW! "Build" is the operative word; it's a process and takes time. What you do with your time is crucial. Have you read something today that will inspire you to keep moving forward? How about something that will empower you, sharpen your skillset or, most importantly, something that will strengthen your faith? Are you looking for opportunities to shine? What are you doing to prepare for your next level? Take time to prepare for your week. Know the difference between busy work and actual client work.

Strategy is necessary when developing a business. It's important to be specific. Vital information and tactical methods are good components of a successful plan. Be intentional, your vision/dream/goal is not a random thought.

You were created for a specific purpose. Don't minimize your gifts and talents. Put in the work, do your research or Vision Concepts, LLC can help you. The first step is acknowledging your untapped potential and purpose. You were designed to do something greater. This will require a shift in your mindset and openness to change. Vision Concepts, LLC enjoys helping individuals embrace and align with their divine purpose and develop strategic ways to monetize their passion.

## Breaking Through Barriers in Business

Have you discovered the difficulties of 'barriers to entry' in your industry? No matter which approach you use to stake your claim in the market, your competitors seems to soar ahead of you every time. You may say to yourself "My services are just as good and maybe better" or "What are they doing that I'm not?" You may be looking at things from the wrong angle. Don't limit your thinking.

This reminds me of a recent trip to a recreation center. My intention was to walk on a trail or path. I couldn't see one, but as I started to leave, I saw someone walking on the other side of the field (right side of picture below). I looked to the left, saw a patch of cement (on the left side).

Determined to take my walk, I proceeded in that direction and found a fitness station, outdoor exercise equipment for public use. I eventually located the path, and although it looked like a dead end and I wasn't sure where it would lead me, I took a risk and started walking. Low and behold, along the path leading around the field, I stumbled on a park with a nature reserve and nature trail.

I took a risk and what happened? Not only did I find the walking path and a fitness station, but also a nature reserve and nature trail. So many new resources are now open to me. This will help me succeed in my weight release journey. How is this relevant? It's a good example of not being discouraged if you hit a "barrier to entry." The barrier may or may not be as difficult to enter into your market as it appears. Don't limit yourself, research your market and determine the following:

- Is your market untapped?
- Is your niche and target audience so specific that no one is willing to pay for your services?
- Have you obtained proof of market demand by researching competitor's activities (e.g., blogs, books, and podcasts)?

Remember, if your market appears to be saturated and everyone seems to be providing your product or service, don't fret. This could be a good thing; it means there's high demand. However, you will need to differentiate your business from your competitors. Utilize resources such as social media. Blogging and podcasts will also allow you to connect with your potential customers/clients. It will show them how you can provide value and that you have a solution to their problem. It also allows you to gain their trust by showing your expertise. Using these approaches will allow the following to happen:

- Lead generation (building your CRM/database)

- Create a sales funnel (offerings of your product or service to potential customers/clients)

- Turn prospects into customers/clients

Before you do this, make sure you have a system in place to follow through on your promise to serve. You must put in the work to get results. Tap into your passion to help fuel your innovation yet use wisdom. Don't be one-sided; there are so many opportunities on the other side. Oh yeah, and don't get distracted in your discoveries. You may find so many offerings you didn't realize you could provide but remember to focus on one brilliant idea at a time. It's time to cause your 'Barrier to Entry' to be a Breakthrough to Your Success!

> *"When you believe in your dream and your vision, then it begins to attract its own resources. No one was born to be a failure." ~ Dr. Myles Munroe*

## How will you take action on your vision?

Jacqueline Turnbo

# My 30-Day Accountability Plan

## My 60-Day Accountability Plan

# My Goals for the Next Quarter

## My Goals for the Next Six Months

## My Goals for the Next Year

## Where I See Myself Five Years From Now

# Conclusion

*N*ow that you've read this, are ready for a mindset shift? It is time to walk in your gifts and calling. Don't hesitate to embrace your divine purpose. We have covered some pros and cons, things required to shift your mindset. Hopefully, something was said that will help push you towards your divide destiny. Don't allow doubt, fear, and procrastination to prevent you from being intentional about your entrepreneurial journey.

Don't be afraid of success and allow fear to hinder your progress. Keep moving forward with faith. Enter entrepreneurship with the idea that you are designed to carry out the vision that God has given you. Trust and embrace the process, don't be afraid to take risks but use wisdom before you proceed. Allow God to guide you along your journey so you can fulfill your divine purpose and serve those you've been assigned to serve. Don't compare yourself with others but allow their fruitfulness to motivate you. Keep moving, growing and developing into the true visionary that you are.

There is something that only you were created to do. Yes, there's others in your industry that may have a similar platform, but they cannot do it like you can. Don't miss the opportunity to live on purpose and walk out God's divine plan for your life. Don't let it be said that you did not fulfill your assignment. When you see someone doing the things that God whispered in your spirit and tugged at your heart to do, don't feel defeated or give up. Yes, you missed the opportunity in that moment; moving forward be determined to act on the opportunities given to you and walk in your divine purpose.

God has designed something specifically for you. He is the Master Architect, accept the blueprint that He has laid out for you. You have a choice to live the life you/others design or live the life that was created for you. Which will you choose? Will you live this life randomly not taking risks, showcasing your gifts and talents? Or helping individuals that need your product/service, your vision?

Welcome God into all your decisions for He knows your outcome. Remember, He is the Divine Architect. It is not your job to design your future but to carry it out according to your Creator's divine design. God has endless resources for you, tap into them and live from the overflow because you are filled with promise and destined to be a blessing to others.

This is phase one of *From Wantrepreneur ™ to Entrepreneur Mindset Shift Blueprint to Your Divine Purpose."* Allow phase one to help you prepare for phase two by positioning yourself and posturing your heart for greater. As you prepare to step into entrepreneurship or have a different perspective about entrepreneurship, you will be open to endless possibilities and growth. Your territory will expand as you make room by ridding yourself of self-sabotaging behaviors. As you put in the necessary work and recognize it takes time to build a viable, profitable and sustainable business, you will see progress.

> *"Make measurable progress in reasonable time."*
> *~ Jim Rohn*

Accountability is one important component of a mindset shift. Being in a community that helps you stay accountable can also help you stay focused. We invite you to join the **Your Accountability Group.** It's a free closed Facebook group. Go to **bit.ly/yaccountability to join.**

*Check out other books by Jacqueline Turnbo,
purchase on Amazon:*

A Creek Between Two Cities: #WarWithIn
and
A Creek Between Two Cities: #WarWithIn
Breakthrough Barriers Workbook

*Coming in 2019!*

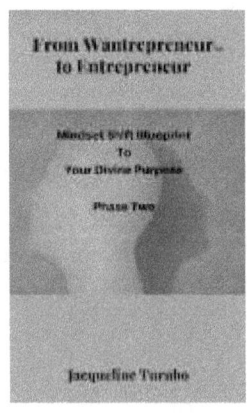

www.ingramcontent.com/pod-product-compliance
Lightning Source LLC
Chambersburg PA
CBHW071207220526
45468CB00002B/535